I0608489

PEACE BEYOND
THE CLOUDS

PEACE BEYOND
THE CLOUDS

N. A. CHEATHAM

Copyright © 2022 by N. A. Cheatham
All rights reserved. This book or any portion thereof may not be reproduced or used in any manner whatsoever without the express written permission of the publisher except for the use of brief quotations in a book review.

Limits of Liability and Disclaimer of Warranty

The author and publisher shall not be liable for your misuse of this material. The purpose of this book is to entertain. The author and publisher do not guarantee anyone following these techniques, suggestions, tips, ideas, or strategies will become successful. The author and publisher shall have neither liability nor responsibility to anyone with respect to any loss or damage caused, or alleged to be caused, directly or indirectly by the information contained in this book. Views expressed in this publication do not necessarily reflect the views of the publisher.

Printed in the United States of America
Keen Vision Publishing, LLC
www.publishwithKVP.com
ISBN: 978-1-955316-11-8

Just for you, the reader. Be at ease.
We are on this journey of life together. No matter what
it look likes, we are all doing our best to figure it out.
You are not alone.

CONTENTS

ONE LONG NIGHT

As the sun begins to drift away into the darkness
And the moon starts to illuminate the dark sky
The more this bottle filled with poison calls one's name
Wishing the precious memories that were once shared
Never show themselves again due to always leaving a stain

Trying desperately to forget the small details of another
While tightly holding onto something called sanity
One must cope with the end of a beautiful beginning
Though the uncertainty of wellness is the main concern

As the moon shines bright in the darkness as if it was the sun
The effects of this poison begin to take over the body
Can this take away the pain that is deep in the heart and mind
Or, does one need to prepare more bottles for one long night

A MOTIVATION CALLED HUNGER

Growing up in the hood had its rough moments
From having to worry about houses being broken into
To being cautious of the ones who we call friends
And aware of areas during certain times of the day

Though these experiences may seem harsh at first glance
One can still achieve anything they set their minds to
Even if it seems like this thing called society is against them
There is always hope, dedication, and hunger for something better

Something better can be a future one never dreamed of having
For their families that couldn't access much while growing up
And to be an idol to the next generation to strive for greatness
A keystone for anything is possible if the mind is challenged enough

CHOICES V. DECISIONS

As a young boy growing up in a surrounding called the hood
Infinite goals and dreams were the main sources of energy
As well as becoming an inspiration to those that follow after
Though the road has its distractions made to steer one off course
Is there something, at one point, that was done wrong
While creating a blueprint for others to use as a source of ambition
Or was it even one's place to lend a helping hand to those
Who may be considered voiceless and is overlooked
As one battles with these questions, reality begins to sink in
Forming struggles between seeing those without a voice succeed
Or lending a hand to those who may need someone who sees them

INFINITY: THE MUSE

Real love is very hard to come across nowadays
A love so rare and special that it gives off a sense of freedom
Where one can express their true feelings without judgment
Towards one who treats their heart and mind as if it's theirs
With a warmness that lowers all defenses of the heart
Negative thoughts toward this love vanish without a trace
And creates a masterpiece between two that found each other
through experiences and hardships which, at a point, feel like
emptiness
One begins to question if each obstacle thus far has its own
meaning
Preparing for a future filled with a breeze of sweet bliss
With another that makes being in their presence seem like infinity

DIFFERENT WAVELENGTHS

At one time, the thought of being on the same path felt real
Where vibes seemed pure and flowed like waterfalls
Though things appeared blissful from others' view
The constant struggle in communication became a battlefield

As frustration continued to target and take over the mind
The thought of "disappointment" began to intertwine with the
present
Due to coping with the reality of finally finding something rare
But too rare to take the same steps one was already prepped for

While the outside noise buzzed in the eardrum frequently
A heart once cased in steel and locked now exposed to the wicked
Falling prey to all temptations with a beautiful smile without a
warning
Of an aura once present that felt copied and owned by different
wavelengths

BITTERSWEET ENDING

What did you expect to happen in this situation
That feelings were going to be put to the side
While forgiving you and not thinking about the damage
In which you'll bring up the past as an escape route

But bringing up the past won't change the hurt and sorrow
A pain that was once locked away in the deepest room of the mind
Unlocked with ease while adding fuel to a flame called the present
Causing a massive argument with no sign of end and peace

With mistakes from both parties being brought from their shadows
And tensions that once flared rapidly began to fall from their peak
The thought of progressing without you begins to flourish in the
mind
Becoming clear as a book titled "Us" with two lines left to the
ending

A VIBE CALLED YOU

As one looks back at the timeline of our once joyous journey
Curiosity, however, about the memories once shared begins to sprout
To draw a conclusion as to why "we" came to an abrupt tragic end
Or, just maybe to hold onto a chance of our paths crossing again

Did she feel the same electric energy when our eyes met for the first time
Or, was it the chemistry created during our first conversation that felt like forever
More questions begin to appear as they flowed frequently after one another
As the regret towards a relationship that seemed like yesterday quickly vanished

Should one have followed her lead more often in hopes of building a future together
As the sense of happiness is worn outside of the body as she's by our side infinitely
Though in reality, the ending of things gave one a taste of something to search for
As her vibes presented a clue to the type of future one must strive for with another

WHEN THE STARS ARE OUT

As the once bright sky begins to fade into the darkness slowly
A pleasant feeling of peacefulness and calmness flows along with
the wind
One begins to ask another, "What is it that catches your eyes first?
Or the thought that pops up in your head as the stars form?"

Is it the beauty of the stars' patterns and formations they take
As they appear, the longer the sun falls into a distant slumber
Or is it the calmness in the atmosphere that one never felt before
As thoughts of being with another who gives off the same sense of
peace

Even the memories of past "ships" may circulate through the mind
As the thoughts of being around them resemble what home should
feel like
Just to hold onto that feeling and never let it retreat again
As the stars admire the view of two individuals who create a scenery
filled with joy

FATHER

Looking back at a childhood once lived
There were things that could not be controlled
One being a father not around daily
With other father figures being around often
Causing blame to be placed on oneself at a young age
Due to a memory that seemed like a constant nightmare
Once reality kicked in, one had to cope with the fact
That an everyday relationship with a father not close
Became hard for a young soul to deal with while growing
While the father was present but often in a phonebook
Years pass and the once childhood became a distant travel
A father-son relationship became strong due to understanding
Of a father's struggle with a thing called Life
A thing that nothing prepares you for until it's too late
As one uses previous lessons from the father and their own
One sees their own goals for a future that is unknown but already
written

THE MIND

Reality makes one realize that most have tough routes to success
Some come from areas considered impoverished
Where one has to learn about Life early
While others encounter life changing events
That leave something called Permanent Scars
However there is always one special ingredient
To their success that is constantly overlooked
Which is the desire to become better
Than their current situations in life
A desire that consists of several ways
With one being able to use their situations
As an inspiration in order to create
A better establishment for their loved ones
Or making a stand amongst themselves
To not stoop as low as before ever again
Which is why the mind is considered
A beautiful masterpiece of this struggle called Life
As long as goals are established frequently
And plans are created to achieve them
One has the absolute power to become
And accomplish anything they truly desire
By a path of achievements being born
Based on a powerful weapon called The Mind

MARIA

As raindrops continuously fall from the clouded sky
She is the only thought that lingers on one's conscious
With the irritation which was expressed on her face
Along with an angry demeanor while stating she was done

Done with the ups and downs during the existence of our union
One tries to believe things will roll over and refresh with space
But the nightmare of her absence feels more and more like quicksand
As the emptiness in our "ship" caused one to sink more without her

The fact that my queen, companion, soul, and heart may finally be done
With the history, bond, and happiness which was created from scratch
And the essence of our creation of love seems more like a joke without the other
The outlook of the journey thus far replays itself while mapping out the mistakes

Inconsistent actions and the lack of affection seem to be the main issues
She wanted to be the first thought, the first choice, and the first consideration
But instead became the last option due to a downfall called communication
Which was missing throughout our time while making decisions as the alpha

Not once did the thought of her opinion sprint across the mind for our future
The same future that ignited during the night and became ashes

The thought of a day without her feels as if the heart itself cried with every beat
Along with the willingness to change starts to swell amongst the core

One continues to express themselves in a note of regret and mistakes
The thought of forgiveness begins to fill the mind with lots of uncertainty
As the future of the history once created is now in our sweet, sweet Maria's hands

INFLUENTIAL ROLE MODEL

Was there ever someone whom one could rely on
While sprouting throughout any stage of life
With any questions, concerns, or guidance
Throughout this chaotic world at anytime
Or maybe even one stepped up to play this role
For another who needed the support
Perhaps for a cousin, sibling, or friend
That felt lonely and afraid due to traumas
One can uplift another's day without even knowing
That their guidance reached that individual's life
Even if they are considered an enemy of the present
Everyone needs that "Food for Thought" periodically
That precious moment to see the greater aspect of life
That offers an infinity of opportunities in different forms
With the mindset to look out for our brothers
And sisters, even those of different pigmentations
To see a joyous expression upon their once gloomed faces
Due to the growth to succeed by one little gentle push
A push towards greatness from someone who's an expected
Or even an unexpected Influential Role Model

MISSING PIECE TO A PUZZLE CALLED LOVE

Ever met someone whose exact presence
And aroma caused a unique experience
As if time decided to pause for a quick moment
With things in the background slowly vanishing
Due to the chemistry formulating from a bond
In which a fresh meeting felt extremely rare
Questions begin to attack the mental frame
Causing the mind to suffer from nervousness
From finally being on the verge of happiness
While experiencing a triumph called joy daily
As if we were the clouds in the big blue sky
That finally found one another and became one
While traveling along with the flow of the wind
With no sense of direction but only to be with her
Even if the destination leads toward a clouded disaster
Soon as an ingredient called happiness began to digest
Within the body, a nasty aftertaste of bitterness appeared
quickly becoming a virus that targeted the mind
As the glimpse of an infinite paradise slowly crumbled
Even while leading the hunt for these precious memories
Of a joy that disappeared without even a trace to follow
The thought of a paradise that doesn't stay felt strange
Giving the mind and body a sense of false hope
As thoughts begin to flood the mind while the virus fades
The feeling of something that was nothing but gimmicks
Though without realization, one failed to understand
The discovery of the missing piece to the puzzle called love

A FLAME TOO STRONG

What would you consider to be your motivation to succeed in life
Is it be family members and friends you hold dear to the heart
Or, a mentor that was established ever since your adolescence
If that is the case in your story of essence, then the "how's" and
"why's" matter
Another question starts to brew by stating, "What makes you so
strong?"
Cause when others are in a room along with you, they should see
your aura
An aura that tells the stories of one without uttering a single word
That is when one is at the point in life where they possess a flame
that's strong
Strong enough to produce a flame that spreads as quick as
wildfires
Where in short, the flames are a symbol of something one calls
wisdom
While the wildfire becomes the enrichment of one's influence on
others
Showing the strength of a person's battle with disparity along their
journey
See, the more wisdom one swells up in their core and spirit
throughout life
The stronger one's flames become over time without hesitation
While spreading knowledge to others, causing wildfires too strong
to extinguish

JUST LIKE THE CLOUDS

As I relax upon the back of this body of metal
While all of my focus pinpoints on the sky above
Watching the clouds travel among the breeze of wind
Wondering why the world cannot be as peaceful as them

Can such a thing called love be as calm as these clouds
Or become as undecided as a scale filled with mistrust
I become puzzled as countless inquiries continue to rise
From something that seems so peaceful yet can erupt quickly

No matter how the infinite changes in my surroundings
The mentality of peace will never waver in my mindset
Just like the clouds in the blue ocean called the sky

MORE DOWN THE ROAD

As the wind courses through its surroundings with a Virginia breeze
One looks back on their journey thus far and their achievements
While queries start to formulate, one stands out the most
"What more is there left to accomplish?" continues to circulate
through the mind
From achievements such as having a degree while trying to make a
name for themselves
Only to feel stuck in an abyss with no light to guide one toward a
better destination
Or the friends met along the road that felt more like family based
on the strong bonds
Though the feeling of "What if they're accessible permanently?"
due to unexpected tragedies
Even not having children yet while running a steady race against
time itself feels tough
Due to there being no partner to be the main supporter while in this
tight race of life
With questions of possibly creating their own foundation to
continue a legacy
But to get past the hurdle of a partner's true motives towards one's
heart and mind
Soon realization blossoms from the very depths of intelligence in
one's body
No matter what may be accomplished so far along someone's
travels through life
There is plenty of room for more to achieve as there is more written
to your story
As each book has chapters where the story is the main source of
importance

THOSE WE HOLD DEAR

Once someone is enclosed by people they love, whether friends or family
The thought of losing them never crosses the mind due to living in the moment
But when this impossible occurrence actually becomes a reality
It is one of the toughest periods in someone's life as shock and sadness travel the body
Whether it was a simple passing away or they were taken away over stupidity
The emotions that continue to flow out with no sign of shutting off
Along with the constant memories of the good times one cannot relive ever again
Sprouting any time of the day as one tries their hardest to cherish them like treasure
Never realizing that all these precious memories are as important as life itself
As they are the source of that loved one living through these exact memories
Never wanting to let them go or out of sight again while time runs its course
Whether it is a friend or family member, treat every point in life with them like gold
As the fun times with them eventually end with the hard times without them around
But while we go through these troubled times without them, they are actually still present
Within our memories pushing us forward throughout this shaky world called Life
Those who we hold dear to the heart become the source we need to continue the journey

FOCUSED/DISTRACTIONS

Many people ask why the word "single" is in one's environment
To be quite frank, there is nothing wrong with being single
Due to the time that becomes available to understand oneself
While figuring out goals that lead towards a bright future
Though the absence of "The One" does cross the mind
periodically
Even thoughts of approaching someone who is unavailable
Without any emotion towards their union due to "just because"
But in reality, taking another's queen can come back as a
nightmare
Due to chaos called karma which is created with many faces
So in the "single" environment, there is a preference to stay
respectful
Towards another's situation in order to avoid dealing with karma
Even if there is a connection with a queen whose king isn't
honorable
There will be a time when everything will fall in place due to
patience

LIFE: HEADS OR TAILS

Have you ever taken the time to really think about life
The highs and lows you experience throughout time
The moments where happiness finally puts the body at ease
Or the setbacks of depression that reappear despite progress
The positives in every situation that lightens your day
Or the negatives that become the dark clouds of your path
No matter which moment or period occurs throughout time
You must realize it could become worst than the present
Where another's situation can be considered less suitable to
imagine

ABOUT THE AUTHOR

N.A. Cheatham was born in Richmond, Virginia and later moved to Baton Rouge, Louisiana, where he currently resides. His interest in poetry began in high school. As he started writing more poems he became fully committed to translating thoughts onto paper to help clear his mind of everyday challenges....and the writing continues...

ACKNOWLEDGMENTS

I want to take a moment to thank everyone that played a factor in the creation of this book. Whether it was brainstorming ideas or critiques. I'm grateful for the interactions with others that helped play a big role in this piece. To the readers, hopefully you enjoyed this experience. There is more to come.

Until next time.....

N.A. CHEATHAM

CONNECT WITH THE AUTHOR

Thank you for reading, *Peace Beyond the Clouds*. N.A. Cheatham can't wait to connect with you. Here are a few ways you can contact the author.

FACEBOOK   NILE CHEATHAM
INSTAGRAM   @NILEBEEZY

www.ingramcontent.com/pod-product-compliance
Lightning Source LLC
Chambersburg PA
CBHW031134260626
47153CB00021B/1471